ARIS & PHILLIPS HISPANIC CLASSICS

One River, One Love

Un río, un amor

Poems by Luis Cernuda

Translation, Introduction and Notes by

Philip G. Johnston

Aris & Phillips is an imprint of Oxbow Books

Published in the United Kingdom in 2015 by
OXBOW BOOKS
10 Hythe Bridge Street, Oxford OX1 2EW

and in the United States by
OXBOW BOOKS
1950 Lawrence Road, Havertown, PA 19083

Un Río, un Amor © Herederos de Luis Cernuda 1964;
English translation © Philip Johnston 2015

Hardback Edition: ISBN 978-1-91057-222-1
Paperback Edition: ISBN 978-1-91057-223-8
Digital Edition: ISBN 978-1-91057-224-5

A CIP record for this book is available from the British Library

For a complete list of Aris & Phillips titles, please contact:

UNITED KINGDOM
Oxbow Books
Telephone (01865) 241249
Fax (01865) 794449
Email: oxbow@oxbowbooks.com
www.oxbowbooks.com

UNITED STATES OF AMERICA
Oxbow Books
Telephone (800) 791-9354
Fax (610) 853-9146
Email: queries@casemateacademic.com
www.casemateacademic.com/oxbow

Oxbow Books is part of the Casemate group

Front cover: *Luis Cernuda*. Portrait by Ramón Gaya. Oil on canvas *c.* 1932.
Private collection. Reproduced by kind permission, all rights reserved.

For Suzanne (my 'Birdie')

CONTENTS

TRANSLATOR'S NOTE

The first translation issue associated with this collection concerns its title. Apparently Cernuda initially intended to call it *Cielo sin dueño* (*Heaven without a Master*); then he seemed to favour a title in English *A Little River, A Little Love*, after, it would seem, a song associated with an American Jazzman, one Buddy Van Arlen; finally he settled on *Un río, un amor*. The strong temptation therefore was to translate this final title as *A Little River, A Little Love*. However, since copious research has failed to uncover either that song-title or an artist named Buddy Van Arlen, and since the very literal *A River, A Love* falls flat and somewhat wide of the musical mark set by some of the collection's content, a decision was taken to opt for *One River, One Love*, which is more musical and evocative than either of the alternatives.

The *modus operandi* of this translator is to translate as faithfully as possible to the original: even when, or especially when, the finished product in English seems bizarre, as is only to be expected in the context of a work written on the fringes of Surrealism. Although some of the early poems exhibit the Alexandrine line-form, there is generally no strict line- or rhyme-scheme to observe or represent in translation. Rarely then does the imperative to moderate or to interpret arise, which options would anyway not be reflective of the poet's original intentions.

When lecturing to undergraduates on poetry which is Surrealist or – as in the case of this collection – quasi-Surrealist, this translator is wont to quote Lautréamont's evocation of "the fortuitous encounter on a dissection table of a sewing machine and an umbrella". Students are told that if they have difficulty in fully conceiving of this evocation then they are half-way towards understanding Surrealism and related phenomena. This translation is made and offered in that spirit.

Lastly my thanks to Lydia Capitano, Ryan Dillon, Tara Evans, Pepe García Velasco, Jackie Johnston, Maria Johnston, Rosa León, Clare Litt, Laura Martín, Jonathan Thacker and Angel Yanguas for help and support, and for being there when needed.

Philip G. Johnston
Dublin 2015

INTRODUCTION

The month of November 1963 took a heavy toll on the world of literature: the English novelist Aldous Huxley and the Irish-born writer C. S. Lewis both died on the 22nd of the month; Luis Cernuda pre-deceased them, dying of a heart attack in Mexico City on the 5th. In a sense these deaths were relatively unnoticed because of a monumental murder that happened in Dallas, Texas, also on the 22nd. By a fitting irony, the American connection is rather appropriate in the context of the work presented in this volume.

Born in Seville on 21 September 1902, Luis Cernuda had a tough, disciplinarian military man from Puerto Rico as his father, and a mother who was a native of Seville. He had two older sisters, Amparo and Ana. His father died in 1920, his mother in 1928. Cernuda definitively left Seville in 1928, and from November of that year until June of 1929 he occupied a Spanish language teaching post in Toulouse (he was a *répétiteur de langue espagnole* in the *Ecole Normale*). This change of scene seems to have heralded a change in the man: a sense of freedom emerges (even if it is only feeling free to express his deep awareness of his personal alienation), there are signs of a recognition of his homosexuality, and, perhaps inspired by his Easter vacation in Paris, he begins to write the poems of *One River, One Love*, his third collection. He finishes the work in the summer of 1929, by which time he is living back in Spain.

Against the background of a Spain which he described as "decrepit and decomposing", but also of devotion to Hollywood movies (Gilbert Roland, John Gilbert – whose moustache Cernuda copied – Douglas Fairbanks Jr, Valentino, Chaplin and Keaton), and of Blues and Jazz music, and the Foxtrot, Waltz, Charleston and Tango, and a fondness for French poetry, particularly that of Paul Eluard, six poems from whose *L'amour, la poésie* he had published in translation in the literary magazine *El litoral,* Cernuda produces a dense, varied and challenging collection of multi-themed poetry. He is unquestionably a member of the so-called Generation of 1927, a disparate group of Spanish writers and intellectuals, united in their common desire to pay homage to the great Golden Age poet Luis de Góngora who died in 1627 and to reform modern Spanish art and writing. Cernuda's poetry epitomises the title given to his first Collected Works volume published in 1936: he articulates the struggle between *La Realidad y El Deseo*, that is harsh, hard reality versus dreams of and aspirations to finer things. *One River, One Love* is an emotional and spiritual autobiography.

Apparently for financial reasons, this collection was not published until the appearance of that Collected Works edition in 1936, by which time the title had changed. Its first eight poems were written in Toulouse in April–May 1929; the remaining twenty-two in July–August in Madrid. They appear in order of composition, and so, in some senses, may be said to constitute a diary of Cernuda's psychological state, a spiritual biography.

Alienation is a key concept in this collection, and is nowhere better exemplified than in its first poem, where the protagonist – the "grey man" – is a sad figure, tortured by remorse and cut off from others. He is non-descript, almost ethereal, with an imperceptible presence. His "empty body" renders him something akin to T. S. Eliot's *Hollow Men* , as he barely functions as a marginalised existent in a society which itself is seen as empty, sterile and insensitive and in a world where there is no consolation from a benevolent god, living, as this "grey man" does, "under an implacable sky". Both the Toulouse and the Madrid poems evoke the exclusion of the poetic protagonist (perhaps Cernuda himself): in 'Exile' the indifference of other people is seen as an age-old situation, "Over a river of oblivion, runs the same old song"; and in 'Like the Wind' the lonely errant figure, tortured by a love experience, is racked by rage, anxiety and insomnia, is excluded by others ("he taps vainly on windows") and deprived of an emotional outlet ("his sadness devoid of tears"), in spite of having arrived full of ideals and aspirations ("I came like light"). The title of one of the later poems ('Let's Not Ever Try Love Again') and its final lines ("where no one / Knows anything about anyone, / Where the world ends") say much about the near-nihilism that obtains with regard to meaningful, communicative human relationships; even when one such relationship is alluded to, as happens in the text 'I Do Not Know What to Call Him in My Dreams', it proves to be either irreparably lost in the past or to have been a figment of the poet's imagination.

Indubitably a contributory factor in Luis Cernuda's profound sense of alienation from so- called normal society lay in his being a homosexual. Seville in the 1920s was hardly the ideal location for 'coming out'. However, the death in 1928 of his mother, with whom he lived in the city's *Calle del aire*, saw him able to move out and on: *One River, One Love* sees him beginning, sometimes obliquely, sometimes more openly, to defend the value of homosexual eroticism and love, against a 'straight', patriarchal society. The collection is shot through with gay signifiers: specifically – birds, wings, feathers, clouds, velvet; more generally – night, darkness, insomnia, silence and death. Hands – and severed hands – speak of homosexual frustration, of not being able to touch, and so on. Cernuda contributes to righting the wrong of homosexuality's absence from traditional literary and historical representation and narrative. For example, some of the US poems could also be read as referring to idyllic homoerotic locations. What is sometimes only implicit in this collection becomes much more overt in his next work *Los Placeres Prohibidos* (*The Forbidden Pleasures*).

As depicted in *Un río, un amor*, the harsher side of life (*La Realidad*, to use his own terminology) is omnipresent. By contrast, however, *El Deseo* is also a significant factor: initial boredom in Toulouse, for instance, seems to fire in the poet a desire for some escapist relief – in the shape of longings and fantasies related to the USA, inspired by his predilection for American cinema and music (specifically, Jazz and Blues). There is a run of American poems in the collection beginning with 'I Want to be Alone in the South'. Here Cernuda wishfully evokes the southern states of the USA, which area may be said to be described by him as the very essence of the Blues, since it "cries as it sings" and is so intensely right for the poet that darkness and light are viewed as complete equals. The collection's very next poem 'White Shadows', inspired by Cernuda's viewing in Paris of one of the first 'talking' movies, celebrates, as did the film, the island of Tahiti – but does so in a very Hollywood style involving frolicking lovers, sun-kissed beaches and a world of "banished fate" where everything (including even a gay agenda) will turn out well because the scriptwriter has 'banished' the vicissitudes of 'normal' fate. The ante-penultimate Toulouse poem 'Nevada', inspired almost certainly by a Gary Cooper movie of 1927 which had the selfsame title, sees the most alluring evocation of a totally mythical and idyllic USA, where even same-sex relationships flourish. The poem is short on facts – Nevada is hardly a snowbound locus, and was probably no more accommodating of gay relationships than any other 'straight', ostensibly 'macho' place.

The experienced reader of Cernuda will, however, allow him this small, fantastical indulgence – knowing full well that, characteristically for the poet, such positivity will not be sustained. The remaining American poems in the collection gradually see Cernuda becoming progressively and notably disenchanted with the USA he previously elevated to the pedestal of *locus amoenus*. 'Durango', in spite of its evocation of bellicose, iconically gay warriors, ends with suggestions of sterility, submission and deprivation. 'Daytona', once an ideal location, ends up being evoked as dormant, forgotten and frozen. Two final American poems, 'Sea Flesh' and 'The Song of the West', respectively see Cernuda reflecting on his own figurative mutilation and degradation, and then evoking a catalogue of surreal devastation, destruction and confusion. Gradually and – it can be assumed – regretfully, Cernuda becomes disillusioned with the idea of vicarious fulfilment through evocations of a mythical America, or, as he puts it at the end of 'Sea Flesh', it is "pointless to conjure up autumn" like some magician.

One of the key issues raised by this collection concerns Cernuda's adherence or otherwise to the principles of Surrealism. We know that his working in bookshops in Seville and Madrid complemented his natural literary curiosity in that regard, and that he read Aragon, Breton, Crevel and Eluard (whose famous line "la terre est bleue comme une orange" was emblematic). In a sense, Surrealist expression, articulating what was chaotic and disordered in ways to which the same two adjectives could be applied, would seem to have been perfectly suited to Cernuda's emotional state of disillusionment, agony and alienation. (The Symbolist landscapes and sentiments of his earlier poetry are no longer adequate to express his *angst*.) The movement's avowed desire to remove barriers between the conscious and subconscious parts of the human mind would also have been apposite. Cernuda may be said to mimic, or flirt with, Surrealist procedures and techniques, but he perhaps never goes far enough into absurdity, nor gives himself completely over to automatic writing, to what Breton called "dictée de la pensée". Readers will decide for themselves just how Surrealist this collection was; but maybe it would be better to refer to its texts exemplifying free-association rather than pure Surrealism, and to Cernuda as a latter-day Romantic, that is to say as an isolated individual assailed by his own heartfelt emotions in a world hostile to his dreams and desires.

Notwithstanding these reservations about claiming too close an association between Cernuda and Surrealism, it must be admitted that the movement itself was identified with revolt or rebellion; the same may be said of *One River, One Love* – or at least of some of its later poems, written in Madrid in August 1929. As evinced in essays he wrote about the era, Cernuda certainly had a revolutionary streak in him; this extended even to his tastes in literature – André Gide's classic homosexual Outsider Lafcadio from *Les Caves du Vatican* was a case in point. In 'All This for Love' Cernuda barely disguises his disdain for what was left of Spanish colonialism and for the Spanish monarchy (specifically the king, Alfonso XIII), railing against "empires founded on a single night, / Monarchies founded on a kiss". He ironizes and criticizes the younger generation in Spain in the mordantly sarcastic 'Sleep, Sonny'. However the single most strident poem of social comment and protest is the late 'Are They All Happy?' where Cernuda denounces conventional views of honour, patriotism and sacrifice, uttering his own (almost anarchic) cries for reform and revision of society and of life's values in general. His anti-conformism strikes impressive, muscularly socialist chords; its impact on this poetry is late, but notable; sufficiently so as perhaps to make the reader wish that it had appeared earlier in the collection and more consistently throughout it.

SELECT BIBLIOGRAPHY

Principal edition of Cernuda's complete poems

Cernuda, L. 1993. *Poesía completa, Obra completa*, Vol. 1. Ed. D. Harris and L. Maristany. Madrid: Siruela.

Edition of text on which this translation is based

Cernuda, L. 2005. *Un Río, un Amor / Los Placeres Prohibidos*. Ed. D. Harris. Cátedra, Letras Hispánicas 473, 3rd edn. Madrid: Cátedra.

Books and articles (in English)

Edkins, A. and Harris, D. 1971. *The Poetry of Luis Cernuda*. New York: New York University Press.

Harris, D. 1995. *The Spanish Avant-garde* . Manchester: Manchester University Press.

Harris, D. 1998. *Metal Butterflies and Poisonous Lights: The Language of Surrealism in Lorca, Alberti, Cernuda and Aleixandre*. Fife: La Sirena.

McKinlay, N. C. 1999. *The Poetry of Luis Cernuda: Order in a World of Chaos*. London: Tamesis.

Morris, C. B. 1969. *A Generation of Spanish Poets (1920–1936)*. Cambridge: Cambridge University Press.

Morris, C. B. 1972. *Surrealism and Spain*. Cambridge: Cambridge University Press.

Morris, C. B. (ed.) 1991. *The Surrealist Adventure in Spain*. Ottowa: Dovehouse Editions.

Silver, P. 1965. '*Et In Arcadia Ego*': *A Study of the Poetry of Luis Cernuda*. London: Tamesis.

Summerhill, S. J. 1978. *Un Río, un Amor*: Cernuda's Flirtation with Surrealism, *Journal of Spanish Studies* VI, 2, 131–157.

ONE RIVER, ONE LOVE

UN RÍO, UN AMOR

REMORDIMIENTO EN TRAJE DE NOCHE

Un hombre gris avanza por la calle de niebla;
No lo sospecha nadie. Es un cuerpo vacío;
Vacío como pampa, como mar, como viento,
Desiertos tan amargos bajo un cielo implacable.

Es el tiempo pasado, y sus alas ahora
Entre la sombra encuentran una pálida fuerza;
Es el remordimiento, que de noche, dudando,
En secreto aproxima su sombra descuidada.

No estrechéis esa mano. La yedra altivamente
Ascenderá cubriendo los troncos del invierno.
Invisible en la calma el hombre gris camina.
¿No sentís a los muertos? Mas la tierra está sorda.

REMORSE IN A DINNER JACKET

A grey man advances along a hazy street;
No one suspects a thing. His is an empty body;
Empty as the pampas, as the sea, as the wind,
Such bitter deserts under an implacable sky.

This is the flight of times past whose wings just now
Encounter a pallid force amidst the shadows;
This is remorse which, by night, cast down by doubt,
Secretly approaches his neglected shadow.

Do not take that hand. The ivy will haughtily
Rise to cover winter's trunk.
Invisible in the calmness the grey man goes on his way.
Though the earth is muffled, don't you sense the dead?

QUISIERA ESTAR SOLO EN EL SUR

Quizá mis lentos ojos no verán más el sur
De ligeros paisajes dormidos en el aire,
Con cuerpos a la sombra de ramas como flores
O huyendo en un galope de caballos furiosos.

El sur es un desierto que llora mientras canta,
Y esa voz no se extingue como pájaro muerto;
Hacia el mar encamina sus deseos amargos
Abriendo un eco débil que vive lentamente.

En el sur tan distante quiero estar confundido.
La lluvia allí no es más que una rosa entreabierta:
Su niebla misma ríe, risa blanca en el viento.
Su oscuridad, su luz son bellezas iguales.

I WANT TO BE ALONE IN THE SOUTH

Perhaps my waning eyes will never again see the south
Made of light landscapes sleeping in the air,
With bodies in the shade of branches like flowers
Or in flight in the gallop of wild horses.

The south is a desert which cries as it sings,
And that voice is not smothered like a dead bird;
Seaward it guides its bitter desires
Announcing a feeble echo that lives barely.

In the, oh, so distant south I wish to be subsumed.
There, rain is merely a half-open rose:
The very mist laughs, white laughter in the wind.
Darkness and light are of the same beauty.

SOMBRAS BLANCAS

Sombras frágiles, blancas, dormidas en la playa,
Dormidas en su amor, en su flor de universo,
El ardiente color de la vida ignorando
Sobre un lecho de arena y de azar abolido.

Libremente los besos desde sus labios caen
En el mar indomable como perlas inútiles;
Perlas grises o acaso cenicientas estrellas
Ascendiendo hacia el cielo con luz desvanecida.

Bajo la noche el mundo silencioso naufraga;
Bajo la noche rostros fijos, muertos, se pierden.
Sólo esas sombras blancas, oh blancas, sí, tan blancas.
La luz también da sombras, pero sombras azules.

WHITE SHADOWS

Fragile, white shadows, sleeping on the beach,
Sleeping in love, in their flower-like universe,
Ignorant of life's ardent colour
On a bed of sand and of banished fate.

Kisses fall freely from their lips
Into the indomitable sea like unwanted pearls;
Grey pearls or maybe ashen stars
Rising to the heavens in fading light.

Under nightfall the silent world is shipwrecked;
Under nightfall fixed, moribund faces are lost.
Only those white shadows, so white, oh, so white.
The light also casts its shadows, but they are blue.

CUERPO EN PENA

Lentamente el ahogado recorre sus dominios
Donde el silencio quita su apariencia a la vida.
Transparentes llanuras inmóviles le ofrecen
Árboles sin colores y pájaros callados.

Las sombras indecisas alargándose tiemblan,
Mas el viento no mueve sus alas irisadas;
Si el ahogado sacude sus lívidos recuerdos,
Halla un golpe de luz, la memoria del aire.

Un vidrio denso tiembla delante de las cosas,
Un vidrio que despierta formas color de olvido;
Olvidos de tristeza, de un amor, de la vida,
Ahogados como un cuerpo sin luz, sin aire, muerto.

Delicados, con prisa, se insinúan apenas
Vagos revuelos grises, encendiendo en el agua
Reflejos de metal o aceros relucientes,
Y su rumbo acuchilla las simétricas olas.

Flores de luz tranquila despiertan a lo lejos,
Flores de luz quizá, o miradas tan bellas
Como pudo el ahogado soñarlas una noche,
Sin amor ni dolor, en su tumba infinita.

A su fulgor el agua seducida se aquieta,
Azulada sonrisa asomando en sus ondas.
Sonrisas, oh miradas alegres de los labios;
Miradas, oh sonrisas de la luz triunfante.

BODY IN PAIN

Slowly the drowned man surveys his domains
Where silence deprives life of its appearance.
Motionless, transparent plains show him
Colourless trees and silent birds.

Indecisive shadows tremble while extending,
But the wind does not move their iridescent wings;
If the drowned man stirs his livid memories,
He will find a stroke of light, the air's memory.

A dense pane of glass trembles before things,
A glass which stirs forms the colour of oblivion;
Forgotten things of sadness, of love, of life,
Drowned like a body without light and air, truly dead.

Delicate, hastily, there scarcely insinuate themselves
Some vague, grey stirrings, lighting in the water
Reflections of shining metal and steel,
Whose pathway scythes through the symmetrical waves.

Flowers of tranquil light awaken in the distance,
Flowers of light perhaps, or gazes so beautiful
That the drowned man can one night conjure them up in dreams,
Shorn of love and pain, in his infinite tomb.

In its brilliance the seduced water calms,
With a bluish smile showing on its waves.
Smiles, joyful gazes of the lips;
Gazes, smiles of the triumphant light.

Desdobla sus espejos la prisión delicada;
Claridad sinuosa, errantes perspectivas.
Perspectivas que rompe con su dolor ya muerto
Ese pálido rostro que solemne aparece.

Su insomnia maquinal el ahogado pasea.
El silencio impasible sonríe en sus oídos.
Inestable vacío sin alba ni crepúsculo,
Monótona tristeza, emoción en ruinas.

En plena mar al fin, sin rumbo, a toda vela;
Hacia lo lejos, más, hacia la flor sin nombre.
Atravesar ligero como pájaro herido
Ese cristal confuso, esas luces extrañas.

Pálido entre las ondas cada vez más opacas
El ahogado ligero se pierde ciegamente
En el fondo nocturno como un astro apagado.
Hacia lo lejos, sí, hacia el aire sin nombre.

The delicate prison splits its reflections;
Sinuous clarity, shifting perspectives.
Perspectives broken with deadened pain
By that pale visage that appears solemn.

The drowned man parades his mechanical insomnia.
The impassive silence smiles in his ears.
Unstable void with neither dawn nor dusk,
Monotonous sadness, shattered emotion.

On the open sea at last, rudderless, at full tilt;
Towards the distance, indeed, towards the nameless flower.
Lightly traversing, like a wounded bird,
That confused glass, those strange lights.

Pallid among the evermore opaque waves
The slight drowned man is blindly lost
In the nocturnal depths like an extinguished star.
Towards the distance, yes, towards the nameless air.

DESTIERRO

Ante las puertas bien cerradas,
Sobre un río de olvido, va la canción antigua.
Una luz lejos piensa
Como a través de un cielo.
Todos acaso duermen,
Mientras él lleva su destino a solas.

Fatiga de estar vivo, de estar muerto,
Con frío en vez de sangre,
Con frío que sonríe insinuando
Por las aceras apagadas.

Le abandona la noche y la aurora lo encuentra,
Tras sus huellas la sombra tenazmente.

EXILE

By the tightly shut doors,
Over a river of oblivion, runs the same old song.
In the distance a light muses
As though through the heavens.
Everyone is probably sleeping,
While he carries his destiny alone.

He tires of being alive, of being dead,
Beset by a chill where blood should course,
By a chill that smiles as it insinuates
Through the dank pavements.

The night abandons him and the dawn picks him up,
Doggedly in his wake is the shadow.

NEVADA

En el Estado de Nevada
Los caminos de hierro tienen nombres de pájaro,
Son de nieve los campos
Y de nieve las horas.

Las noches transparentes
Abren luces soñadas
Sobre las aguas o tejados puros
Constelados de fiesta.

Las lágrimas sonríen,
La tristeza es de alas,
Y las alas, sabemos,
Dan amor inconstante.

Los árboles abrazan árboles,
Una canción besa otra canción;
Por los caminos de hierro
Pasa el dolor y la alegría.

Siempre hay nieve dormida
Sobre otra nieve, allá en Nevada.

NEVADA

In the State of Nevada
The railway tracks have birds' names,
The fields are snow-clad
As are the passing hours.

The transparent night-time
Opens dreamt-of lights
On the pure waterways and roofs,
Festively decked.

Tears smile,
Sadness sprouts wings,
And wings, we know,
Mean fickle love.

Trees hug trees,
One song kisses another;
Along the railway tracks
Run pain and joy.

There's always snow sleeping
On other snow, over there in Nevada.

COMO EL VIENTO

Como el viento a lo largo de la noche,
Amor en pena o cuerpo solitario,
Toca en vano a los vidrios,
Sollozando abandona las esquinas;

O como a veces marcha en la tormenta,
Gritando locamente,
Con angustia de insomnio,
Mientras gira la lluvia delicada;

Sí, como el viento al que un alba le revela
Su tristeza errabunda por la tierra,
Su tristeza sin llanto,
Su fuga sin objeto;

Como él mismo extranjero,
Como el viento huyo lejos.
Y sin embargo vine como luz.

LIKE THE WIND

Like the wind throughout the night,
Love in pain or a lonely body,
He taps vainly on windows,
Sobbing he abandons the street-corners;

Or as sometimes he walks in the storms,
Shouting madly,
With sleepless anguish,
While the delicate rain reels around;

Yes, like the wind to which a dawn reveals
His errant sadness on this earth,
His sadness devoid of tears,
His rudderless flight;

Like himself an outsider,
Like the wind I flee far.
And yet I came like light.

DECIDME ANOCHE

La presencia del frío junto al miedo invisible
Hiela a gotas oscuras la sangre entre la niebla
Entre la niebla viva, hacia la niebla vaga
Por un espacio ciego de rígidas espinas.

Con vida misteriosa quizá los hombres duermen
Mientras desiertos blancos representan el mundo;
Son espacios pequeños como tímida mano,
Silenciosos, vacíos bajo una luz sin vida.

Sí, la tierra está sola, bien sola con sus muertos
Al acecho quizá de inerte transeúnte
Que sin gestos arrostre su látigo nocturno;
Mas ningún cuerpo viene ciegamente soñando.

El dolor también busca, errante entre la noche,
Tras la sombra fugaz de algún gozo indefenso;
Y sus pálidos pasos callados se entrelazan,
Incesante fantasma con mirada de hastío.

Fantasma que desfila prisionero de nadie,
Falto de voz, de manos, apariencia sin vida,
Como llanto impotente por las ramas ahogado
O repentina fuga estrellada en un muro.

Sí, la tierra está sola; a solas canta, habla,
con una voz tan débil que no la alcanza el cielo;·
canta risas o plumas atravesando espacio
bajo un sol calcinante reflejado en la arena.

TELL ME LAST NIGHT

The presence of cold beside invisible fear
Freezes blood to dark drops in the mist,
In the vivid mist, towards the vague mist
Through a blind space of rigid thorns.

With a mysterious life perhaps men sleep
While blank deserts represent the world;
They are small spaces like a hesitant hand,
Silent, empty under a lifeless light.

Yes, the earth is alone, truly alone with its dead,
Lying in wait perhaps for some lifeless passer-by
Who placidly faces up to his nocturnal lashing;
But no human form comes along blindly dreaming.

Pain is also searching, errant in the night,
After the fleeting shadow of some helpless pleasure;
And its soft, quiet steps blend into each other,
A ceaseless ghost with a look of weariness.

A ghost that passes by as no one's prisoner,
Deprived of voice, of hands, a lifeless appearance,
Like an impotent wail drowned in branches
Or a sudden flight shattered on a wall.

Yes, the earth is alone; alone it sings, it speaks,
with a voice so frail that the sky cannot reach it;
it sings of laughter or plume traversing space
under a burning sun reflected on the sand.

Es íntima esa voz, sólo para ella misma;
Al exterior la sombra presta asilo inseguro.
Un grito acaso pasa disfrazado con luces,
Luchando vanamente contra el miedo y el frío.

¿Dónde palpita el hielo? Dentro, aquí, entre la vida,
En un centro perdido de apagados recuerdos,
De huesos ateridos en donde silba el aire,
Con un rumor de hojas que se van una a una.

Sus plumas moribundas van extendiendo la niebla
Para dormir en tierra un ensueño harapiento,
Ensueño de amenazas erizado de nieve,
Olvidado en el suelo, amor menospreciado.

Se detiene la sangre por los miembros de piedra
Como al coral sombrío fija el mar enemigo,
Como coral helado en el cuerpo deshecho,
En la noche sin luz, en el cielo sin nadie.

That voice is intimate, for itself alone;
Outside the shadow gives uncertain shelter.
A cry perchance is uttered disguised by lights,
Struggling in vain against fear and cold.

Where does ice throb? Here, within, in life,
In a lost centre of extinguished memories,
Of numb bones where the air whistles
With the noise of leaves that depart one by one.

Its moribund plume extends the mist
To sleep on land a ragged dream,
A dream of threats that bristles with snow,
Forgotten on the soil, a despised love.

Blood is stemmed in the stone members
As the alien sea clings to the dark coral,
Like frozen coral in a shattered body,
On a dark night, in an uninhabited sky.

OSCURIDAD COMPLETA

No sé por qué, si la luz entra,
Los hombres andan bien dormidos,
Recogiendo la vida su apariencia
Joven de nuevo, bella entre sonrisas.

No sé por qué he de cantar
O verter de mis labios vagamente palabras,
Palabras de mis ojos,
Palabras de mis sueños perdidos en la nieve.

De mis sueños copiando los colores de nubes,
De mis sueños copiando nubes sobre la pampa.

TOTAL DARKNESS

I know not why, if light enters,
Men are so well slept,
Gathering up life its appearance
Young again, beauteous among smiles.

I know not why I have to sing
Or vaguely shed words from my lips,
Words from my eyes,
Words from my dreams lost in the snow.

From my dreams copying the colours of clouds,
From my dreams copying clouds on the pampas.

HABITACIÓN DE AL LADO

A través de una noche en pleno día
Vagamente he conocido a la muerte.
No la acompaña ningún lebrel;
Vive entre los estanques disecados,
Fantasmas grises de piedra nebulosa.

¿Por qué soñando, al deslizarse con miedo,
Ese miedo imprevisto estremece al durmiente?
Mirad vencido olvido y miedo a tantas sombras blancas
Por las pálidas dunas de la vida,
No redonda ni azul, sino lunática,
Con sus blancas lagunas, con sus bosques
En donde el cazador si quiere da caza al terciopelo.

Pero ningún lebrel acompaña a la muerte.
Ella con mucho amor sólo ama los pájaros,
Pájaros siempre mudos, como lo es el secreto,
Con sus grandes colores formando un torbellino
En torno a la mirada fijamente metálica.

Y los durmientes desfilan como nubes
Por un cielo engañoso donde chocan las manos,
Las manos aburridas que cazan terciopelos o nubes descuidadas.

Sin vida está viviendo solo profundamente.

THE ROOM NEXT DOOR

Over a night in plain daylight
I have vaguely come to know death.
No greyhound accompanies her;
She lives in dried up ponds,
Grey ghosts of nebulous stone.

Why is it that in dreams, sliding along in terror,
This unforeseen fear makes the sleeper shudder?
Look at vanquished oblivion and fear in so many white shadows
Over the pale dunes of life,
A life neither rounded nor blue, but lunatical,
With its white lagoons, with its woods
Where the hunter if he so wishes chases velvet.

But no greyhound accompanies death.
She with a real love only loves birds,
Birds that are always mute, as is the secret,
With its great colours forming a whirlwind
Round the fixed metallic gaze.

And the sleepers file by like clouds
Through a deceptive sky where hands collide,
The weary hands that hunt velvet or neglected clouds.

Lifeless it is living profoundly alone.

ESTOY CANSADO

Estar cansado tiene plumas,
Tiene plumas graciosas como un loro,
Plumas que desde luego nunca vuelan,
Mas balbucean igual que loro.

Estoy cansado de las casas,
Prontamente en ruinas sin un gesto;
Estoy cansado de las cosas,
Con un latir de seda vueltas luego de espaldas.

Estoy cansado de estar vivo,
Aunque más cansado sería el estar muerto;
Estoy cansado del estar cansado
Entre plumas ligeras sagazmente,
Plumas del loro aquel tan familiar o triste,
El loro aquel del siempre estar cansado.

I AM TIRED

Being tired has feathers,
It has graceful feathers like a parrot,
Feathers which of course do not take flight,
But chatter as a parrot does.

I am tired of houses,
Quickly in ruins without a sign;
I am tired of things,
Which, with a lash of silk, then have their backs turned.

I am tired of being alive,
Although it would be even more tiresome to be dead;
I am tired of being tired
Sagely amidst light feathers,
Feathers of that so familiar or sad parrot,
That parrot of constant tiredness.

EL CASO DEL PÁJARO ASESINADO

Nunca sabremos, nunca,
Por qué razón un día
Esas luces temblaron levemente;
Fue una llorosa espuma,
Una brisa más grande,
Sólo las olas saben.

Por eso hoy muestran desdeñosas
Su color de miradas,
Su color ignorante todavía, aunque un recuerdo
Les cante algo, algo levemente.

Fue un pájaro quizá asesinado;
Nadie sabe. Por nadie
O por alguien quizá triste en las piedras,
En los muros del cielo.

Mas de ello hoy nada se sabe.
Sólo un temblor de luces levemente,
Un color de miradas en las olas o en la brisa;
También, acaso, un miedo.
Todo, es verdad, inseguro.

THE CASE OF THE MURDERED BIRD

We will never, ever know
Why one day
Those lights flickered slightly;
It was a tearful spray,
A bigger breeze,
Only the waves know.

So today, disdainfully, they show
Their colour of gazes,
Their as yet unknown colour, although a memory
Sings to them of something, rather lightly.

It was a bird, perhaps murdered;
No one knows. By no one
Or perhaps by someone sad in stones,
In heaven's walls.

But about it today nothing is known.
Only a shimmer of lights gently,
A colour of gazes on the waves or in the breeze;
Also, perhaps, fear.
Everything, it's true, is uncertain.

DURANGO

Las palabras quisieran expresar los guerreros,
Bellos guerreros impasibles,
Con el mañana gris abrazado, como un amante,
Sin dejarles partir hacia las olas.

Por la ventana abierta
Muestra el destino su silencio;
Sólo nubes con nubes, siempre nubes
Más allá de otras nubes semejantes,
Sin palabras, sin voces,
Sin decir, sin saber;
Últimas soledades que no aguardan mañana.

Durango está vacío
Al pie de tanto miedo infranqueable;
Llora consigo a solas la juventud sangrienta
De los guerreros bellos como luz, como espuma.

Por sorpresa los muros
Alguna mano dejan revolando a veces;
Sus dedos entreabiertos
Dicen adiós a nadie,
Saben algo quizá ignorado en Durango.

En Durango postrado,
Con hambre, miedo, frío,
Pues sus bellos guerreros sólo dieron,
Raza estéril en flor, tristeza, lágrimas.

DURANGO

Words want to speak of warriors,
Handsome, impassive warriors,
Embracing the grey future, like a beloved,
Without allowing them to head away towards the waves.

Through the open window
Destiny shows its silence;
Nothing but clouds and clouds, unending clouds
Beyond other similar clouds,
No words, no voice,
No saying, no knowing;
The final solitude that does not expect the future.

Durango is empty,
On foot of so much insurmountable pain;
Crying alone to itself the bloodied youth
Of these warriors handsome as light, as sea spray.

By way of a surprise the walls
Sometimes allow the odd hand to float around;
With its half-open fingers
Signalling goodbye to no one,
Knowing something perhaps unknown in Durango.

In Durango, prostrate,
With hunger, fear, cold,
Because its handsome warriors,
A sterile race in flower, brought merely sadness and tears.

DAYTONA

Hubo un día en que el día no engañaba,
En que sus manos tristes no sostenían un cuervo
Indiferente como los labios de la lluvia,
Como el rojizo hastío.

Mas hoy es imposible
Buscar la luz entre barcas nocturnas;
Alguien cortó la piedra en flor,
Sin que pudiera el mundo
Incendiar la tristeza.

Sólo un lugar existe, cuyos días
Nada saben de aquello,
Aunque todo allí sea mortal, el miedo, hasta las plumas;
Mas las olas abrazan
A tanta luz aún viva.

A tanta luz desbordando en la arena,
Desbordando en las nubes, desbordando en el tiempo,
Que dormita sin voz entre las ramas,
Olvidado fantasma con su collar de frío.

Mirad cómo sonríe hacia el amor Daytona.

DAYTONA

There was once a time when day did not deceive,
When its sad hands did not sustain a crow
As indifferent as the rainfall's lips,
As reddish *ennui.*

But now it is impossible
To search for light among ships in the night;
Someone cut the flowering stone,
Without the world
Being able to burn sadness down.

Only one place exists, whose days
Know nothing of that,
Although everything there may well be mortal, with fear,
    to the very feathers;
But the waves embrace
So much still vivid light.

So much light spilling onto the sand,
Into the clouds, spilling onto time itself,
Slumbering voicelessly among the branches,
A forgotten ghost with its cold collar.

Look how Daytona smiles towards love.

DESDICHA

Un día comprendió cómo sus brazos eran
Solamente de nubes;
Imposible con nubes estrechar hasta el fondo
Un cuerpo, una fortuna.

La fortuna es redonda y cuenta lentamente
Estrellas del estío.
Hacen falta unos brazos seguros como el viento,
Y como el mar un beso.

Pero él con sus labios,
Con sus labios no sabe sino decir palabras;
Palabras hacia el techo,
Palabras hacia el suelo,
Y sus brazos son nubes que transforman la vida
En aire navegable.

MISERY

One day he understood how his arms were
Made only of clouds;
It was impossible with clouds to extend to the full
A body, a fortune.

Fortune is rounded and slowly counts
Summer stars.
Some arms as sure and certain as the wind are needed,
And a kiss like the sea,

But he with his lips,
With his lips knows but to say words;
Words to the ceiling,
Words to the floor,
And his arms are clouds which transform life
Into navegable air.

NO INTENTEMOS EL AMOR NUNCA

Aquella noche el mar no tuvo sueño.
Cansado de contar, siempre contar a tantas olas,
Quiso vivir hacia lo lejos,
Donde supiera alguien de su color amargo.

Con una voz insomne decía cosas vagas,
Barcos entrelazados dulcemente
En un fondo de noche,
O cuerpos siempre pálidos, con su traje de olvido
Viajando hacia nada.

Cantaba tempestades, estruendos desbocados
Bajo cielos con sombra,
Como la sombra misma,
Como la sombra siempre
Rencorosa de pájaros estrellas.

Su voz atravesando luces, lluvia, frío,
Alcanzaba ciudades elevadas a nubes,
Cielo Sereno, Colorado, Glaciar del Infierno,
Todas puras de nieve o de astros caídos
En sus manos de tierra.

Mas el mar se cansaba de esperar las ciudades.
Allí su amor tan sólo era un pretexto vago
Con sonrisa de antaño,
Ignorado de todos.

LET'S NOT EVER TRY LOVE

That night the sea was not sleepy.
Tired of telling its story, always telling its story to wave after wave,
It wanted to live somewhere far away,
Where someone might know about its bitter colour.

With an insomniac voice it said vague things,
Ships gently entwined
In pitch-black depths,
Or ever-pallid bodies, clad in oblivion
Travelling towards nothingness.

It sang of storms, of flowing thunder
Beneath shadowed skies,
Like the shadow itself,
Like the shadow always
Resentful of bird-like stars.

Traversing lights, rain, cold, its voice
Reached cities elevated to the clouds,
Serene Sky, Colorado, Hell's Glacier,
All pure with snow or with fallen stars
In its earthy hands.

But the sea wearied of awaiting the cities.
Love there was merely a vague pretext
With a smile from the days of yore,
A love not known by everyone.

Y con sueño de nuevo se volvió lentamente
Adonde nadie
Sabe nada de nadie.
Adonde acaba el mundo.

Sleepy again it slowly turned round
To where no one
Knows anything about anyone.
Where the world ends.

LINTERNA ROJA

Albergue oscuro con mendigos de noche
Abrazando jirones de frío,
Mientras que los grupos inertes, iguales a una flor de lluvia,
Contemplan cómo pasa una sonrisa.

Poseen estos cuerpos miserables
Formas de ojos sin luz o de arena caída;
Vivir, allí canta una voz, si las manos no fallan,
Es alegre como un amor aprisionado.

Esos mendigos son los reyes sin corona
Que buscaron la dicha más allá de la vida,
Que buscaron la flor jamás abierta,
Que buscaron deseos terminados en nubes.

Los cuerpos palidecen como olas,
La luz es un pretexto de la sombra,
La risa va muriendo lentamente,
Y mi vida también se va con ella.

Mas las sombras no son mendigos o coronas,
Son los años de hastío esta noche con vida;
Y mi vida es ahora un hombre melancólico
Sin saber otra cosa que su llanto.

RED LANTERN

Dark refuge with nocturnal beggars
Embracing tatters of cold,
While the motionless groups, like a flower in rain,
Observe how a smile unfolds.

These miserable bodies possess
Forms of eyes without light or of fallen sand;
To live, there a voice sings out, if hands do not fail,
Is joyful as an imprisoned love.

Those beggars are kings without a crown
Who sought happiness beyond life,
Who sought the never-opened flower,
Who sought desires ended up in clouds.

Bodies pale like waves,
Light is a pretext for shadow,
Laughter dies slowly,
And my life too goes with it.

But the shadows are not beggars or crowns,
They are years of weariness on this vivid night;
And my life now is a sad man
knowing nothing else but its lament.

MARES ESCARLATA

Un gemido molusco
Parece nada de importancia;
Mas de noche un gemido son las olas
De mármol encendido,
Corolas fatigadas
O lascivas columnas.

Un gemido no es nada; son los mares
Coronados de otoño
Ante la puerta seca, como cauce
Olvidado de todos,
Su dolor contra un muro.

Un grito acaso pueda ofrecer más encantos,
Con el manto escarlata,
Con el pecho escarlata.

Son los mares, los mares desbordados
Que atraviesan ciudades humeantes.

SCARLET SEAS

A mollusc-like sigh
Seems unimportant;
But by night a sigh is the wave
Of flaming marble,
Weary corollae
Or wanton columns.

A sigh is something; it is sea
Crowned by autumn
In front of the dry door, as a channel
Forgotten by all,
With its pain against a wall.

A cry may well offer more delights,
With the scarlet cloak,
With the scarlet breast.

These are the seas, the overflowing seas
Which cross smoking cities.

RAZÓN DE LAS LÁGRIMAS

La noche por ser triste carece de fronteras.
Su sombra, en rebelión como la espuma,
Rompe los muros débiles
Avergonzados de blancura;
Noche que no puede ser otra cosa sino noche.

Acaso los amantes acuchillan estrellas,
Acaso la aventura apague una tristeza.
Mas tú, noche, impulsada por deseos
Hasta la palidez del agua,
Aguardas siempre en pie quién sabe a cuáles ruiseñores.

Más allá se estremecen los abismos
Poblados de serpientes entre pluma,
Cabecera de enfermos
No mirando otra cosa que la noche
Mientras cierran el aire entre los labios.

La noche, la noche deslumbrante,
Que junto a las esquinas retuerce sus caderas,
Aguardando, quién sabe,
Como yo, como todos.

REASON FOR TEARS

Being sad, night lacks frontiers.
Its shadow, rebelling like sea spray,
Breaks down weak walls
Ashamed of whiteness;
Night which cannot be anything other than night.

Maybe lovers can stab at the stars,
Maybe adventure can extinguish sadness.
But you, night, spurred on by desires
Towards the pallor of water,
Stand there always waiting for who knows which nightingales.

Further away shiver the abysses
Teeming with snakes in the plumage,
Pillows for sick people
Who cannot see anything but the night
While they trap the air between their lips.

Night, dazzling night,
Around street corners swinging her hips,
Waiting, who knows,
Like me, like us all.

TODO ESTO POR AMOR

Derriban gigantes de los bosques para hacer un durmiente,
Derriban los instintos como flores,
Deseos como estrellas,
Para hacer sólo un hombre con su estigma de hombre.

Que derriben también imperios de una noche,
Monarquías de un beso,
No significa nada;
Que derriben los ojos, que derriben las manos como estatuas vacías,
Acaso dice menos.

Mas este amor cerrado por ver sólo su forma,
Su forma entre las brumas escarlata,
Quiere imponer la vida, como otoño ascendiendo tantas hojas
Hacia el último cielo,
Donde estrellas
Sus labios dan a otras estrellas,
Donde mis ojos, estos ojos,
Se despiertan en otros.

ALL THIS FOR LOVE

They tear down giants from the woods to make a sleeper,
They demolish instincts like flowers,
Desires like stars,
To make merely a man with his stigma of being a man.

Let them demolish also empires founded on a single night,
Monarchies founded on a kiss,
It means nothing;
Let them destroy eyes, destroy hands like empty statues,
It means even less.

But this love enclosed to see only its own form,
Its form among the scarlet mists,
Wanting to impose life, like autumn elevating so many leaves
To the high heavens,
Where stars
Proffer their lips to other stars,
Where my eyes, these eyes,
Awake in the gaze of others.

NO SÉ QUÉ NOMBRE DARLE EN MIS SUEÑOS

Ante mi forma encontré aquella forma
En tiempo de crepúsculo,
Cuando las desapariciones
Confunden los colores a los ojos,
Cuando el último amor
Busca el cuerpo postrero.

Una angustia sin fondo aullaba entre las piedras;
Hacia el aire, hombres sordos,
La cabeza olvidada,
Pasaban a lo lejos como libres o muertos;
Vergonzoso cortejo de fantasmas
Con las cadenas rotas colgando de las manos.

La vida puso entonces una lámpara
Sobre muros sangrientos;
El día ya cansado secaba tristemente
Las futuras auroras, remendadas
Como harapos de rey.

La lámpara eras tú,
Mis labios, mi sonrisa,
Forma que hallan mis manos en todo lo que alcanzan.

Si mis ojos se cierran es para hallarte en sueños,
Detrás de la cabeza,
Detrás del mundo esclavizado,
En ese país perdido
Que un día abandonamos sin saberlo.

I DO NOT KNOW WHAT TO CALL HIM IN MY DREAMS

Facing my form I encountered that other form
At the twilight hour,
When disappearances
Confuse colours to the eyes,
When last-in-line love
Seeks the hindmost body.

A limitless anguish howled off the stones:
Towards the air, deaf men,
Their heads forgotten,
Passed in the distance like free or dead men;
A shameful cortege of ghosts
With broken chains hanging from their hands.

Then life cast a light
On bloodied walls;
The tired daylight sadly dried
The coming dawns, mended
Like a king's rags.

You were that light,
My lips, my smile,
A form attained by my hands in all they reach out for.

If my eyes close it is to find you in dreams,
Beyond the human mind,
Beyond this enslaved world,
In that lost land
That one day we abandon without knowing it.

DUERME, MUCHACHO

La rabia de la muerte, los cuerpos torturados,
La revolución, abanico en la mano,
Impotencia del poderoso, hambre del sediento,
Duda con manos de duda y pies de duda;

La tristeza, agitando sus collares
Para alegrar un poco tantos viejos;
Todo unido entre tumbas como estrellas,
Entre lujurias como lunas;

La muerte, la pasión en los cabellos,
Dormitan tan minúsculas como un árbol,
Dormitan tan pequeñas o tan grandes
Como un árbol crecido hasta llegar al suelo.

Hoy sin embargo está también cansado.

SLEEP, SONNY

The rage of death, the tortured bodies,
The revolution, fan in hand,
The impotence of the powerful, the hunger of the thirsty,
Doubt complete with hands and feet;

Sadness, shaking its necklaces
To enliven so many elderly a little;
All together among tombs like stars,
And lusts like moons;

Death and passion in every lock of hair
Doze as minute as a tree,
Doze as small or big
As a tree swollen right to the ground.

Today, however, he is tired as well.

DRAMA O PUERTA CERRADA

La juventud sin escolta de nubes,
Los muros, voluntad de tempestades,
La lámpara, como abanico fuera o dentro,
Dicen con elocuencia aquello no ignorado,
Aquello que algún día débilmente
Ante la muerte misma se abandona.

Hueso aplastado por la piedra de sueños,
¿Qué hacer, desprovistos de salida,
Si no es sobre puente tendido por el rayo
Para unir dos mentiras,
Mentira de vivir o mentira de carne?

Sólo sabemos esculpir biografías
En músicas hostiles;
Sólo sabemos contar afirmaciones
O negaciones, cabellera de noche;
Sólo sabemos invocar como niños al frío
Por miedo de irnos solos a la sombra del tiempo.

DRAMA OR CLOSED DOOR

Youth without an escort of clouds,
Walls, will of storms,
The lamp, as an inner or outer fan,
Articulate eloquently that which is known,
That which one day feebly
Before death gives itself up.

Bone flattened by the stone of dreams,
What's to be done, if, deprived of exit,
It is not on a bridge built by lightning
To unite two lies,
The lie of living or the lie of flesh?

We only know how to sculpt biographies
In hostile music;
We only know how to count affirmations
Or negations, mane of the night;
We only know how to invoke, like children in the cold
For fear of heading off alone ourselves to the shadow of time.

DEJADME SOLO

Una verdad es color de ceniza,
Otra verdad es color de planeta;
Mas todas las verdades, desde el suelo hasta el suelo,
No valen la verdad sin color de verdades,
La verdad ignorante de cómo el hombre suele encarnarse en la nieve.

En cuanto a la mentira, basta decirle «quiero»
Para que brote entre las piedras
Su flor, que en vez de hojas luce besos,
Espinas en lugar de espinas.

La verdad, la mentira,
Como labios azules,
Una dice, otra dice;
Pero nunca pronuncian verdades o mentiras su secreto torcido;
Verdades o mentiras
Son pájaros que emigran cuando los ojos mueren.

LEAVE ME ALONE

One truth is the colour of ash,
Another is the colour of planets;
But all truths, from earth to earth,
Are not worth the truth without true colours,
The truth ignorant of how man becomes incarnate in the snow.

As for lies, the phrase 'I love' is all that is needed
For them to flower among the stones,
Showing kisses instead of leaves,
Thorns in place of thorns.

Truth, lies,
Like blue lips,
One speaks, the other speaks;
But truth or lies never reveal their tortuous secret;
Truth or lies
Are birds that migrate when eyes go dead.

CARNE DE MAR

Dentro de breves días será otoño en Virginia,
Cuando los cazadores, la mirada de lluvia,
Vuelven a su tierra nativa, el árbol que no olvida,
Corderos de apariencia terrible,
Dentro de breves días será otoño en Virginia.

Sí, los cuerpos estrechamente enlazados,
Los labios en la llave más intima,
¿Qué dirá él, hecho piel de naufragio
O dolor con la puerta cerrada,
Dolor frente a dolor,
Sin esperar amor tampoco?

El amor viene y va, mira;
El amor viene y va,
Sin dar limosna a nubes mutiladas,
Por vestidos harapos de tierra,
Y él no sabe, nunca sabrá más nada.

Ahora inútil pasar la mano sobre otoño.

SEA FLESH

In a few short days it will be autumn in Virginia,
When the hunters, with rain-soaked gaze,
Return to their native soil, the tree that does not forget,
Lambs of desperate appearance,
In a few short days it will be autumn in Virginia.

Yes, the tightly entwined bodies,
Lips on the most intimate key,
What will be said by him, shrivelled like shipwrecked skin
Or pained by the closed door,
Pain facing pain,
With no hope either of love?

Love comes and goes, you know;
Love comes and goes,
Giving no alms to mutilated clouds,
As clothing, tatters of earth,
And he does not know, and never will know.

Pointless now to conjure up autumn.

VIEJA RIBERA

Tanto ha llovido desde entonces,
Entonces, cuando los dientes no eran carne, sino días
Pequeños como un río ignorante
A sus padres llamando porque siente sueño
Tanto ha llovido desde entonces,
Que ya el paso se olvida en la cabeza.

Unos dicen que sí, otros dicen que no;
Mas sí y no son dos alas pequeñas,
Equilibrio de un cielo dentro de otro cielo,
Como un amor está dentro de otro,
Como el olvido está dentro del olvido.

Si el suplicio con ira pide fiestas
Entre las noches más viriles,
No haremos otra cosa que apuñalar la vida
Sonreír ciegamente a la derrota,
Mientras los años, muertos como un muerto,
Abren su tumba de estrellas apagadas.

OLD RIVERBANK

It has rained so much since then,
Then, when teeth were not flesh, but small
Days like an unknowing river
Calling to his parents because he feels sleepy,
It has rained so much since then,
That the footstep is now forgotten in the head.

Some say yes, others say no;
But yes and no are two small wings,
The balance of one sky within another,
As one love is within another,
As oblivion is within oblivion.

If angered torment wants to celebrate
On the most virile nights,
We will do nothing more than stab life
Smile blindly at defeat,
While the passing years, dead like a dead man,
Opens its tomb of extinguished stars.

LA CANCIÓN DEL OESTE

Jinete sin cabeza,
Jinete como un niño buscando entre rastrojos
Llaves recién cortadas,
Víboras seductoras, desastres suntuosos,
Navíos para tierra lentamente de carne,
De carne hasta morir igual que muere un hombre.

A lo lejos
Una hoguera transforma en ceniza recuerdos,
Noches como una sola estrella,
Sangre extraviada por las venas un dia,
Furia color de amor,
Amor color de olvido,
Aptos ya solamente para triste buhardilla.

Lejos canta el oeste,
Aquel oeste que las manos antaño
Creyeron apresar como el aire a la luna;
Mas la luna es madera, las manos se liquidan
Gota a gota, idénticas a lágrimas.

Olvidemos pues todo, incluso al mismo oeste;
Olvidemos que un día las miradas de ahora
Lucirán a la noche, como tantos amantes,
Sobre el lejano oeste,
Sobre amor más lejano.

THE SONG OF THE WEST

A headless horseman,
A horseman like a child searching the waste for
Newly cut keys,
Seductive vipers, sumptuous disasters,
Ships slowly bound for land composed of flesh,
Of flesh to the point of death as a man dies.

In the distance
A bonfire renders memories to ash,
Nights like a single star,
Stray blood through the veins one day,
Fury the colour of love,
Love the colour of oblivion,
Fit now only for a sad garret.

Far away sings the west,
That west which hands once
Thought to seize like air to the moon;
But the moon is wooden, hands melt
Drop by drop, just like tears.

So let's forget everything, even the west itself;
Let's forget that one day present gazes
Will shine in the night, like so many lovers,
On the distant west,
On even more distant love.

¿SON TODOS FELICES?

El honor de vivir con honor gloriosamente,
El patriotismo hacia la patria sin nombre,
El sacrificio, el deber de labios amarillos,
No valen un hierro devorando
Poco a poco algún cuerpo triste a causa de ellos mismos.

Abajo pues la virtud, el orden, la miseria;
Abajo todo, todo, excepto la derrota,
Derrota hasta los dientes, hasta ese espacio helado
De una cabeza abierta en dos a través de soledades,
Sabiendo nada más que vivir es estar a solas con la muerte.

Ni siquiera esperar ese pájaro con brazos de mujer,
Con voz de hombre oscurecida deliciosamente,
Porque un pájaro, aunque sea enamorado,
No merece aguardarle, como cualquier monarca
Aguarda que las torres maduren hasta frutos podridos.

Gritemos sólo,
Gritemos a un ala enteramente,
Para hundir tantos cielos,
Tocando entonces soledades con mano disecada.

ARE THEY ALL HAPPY?

The honour of living with honour gloriously,
Patriotism for a non-descript homeland,
Sacrifice, the duty of sallow lips,
Are not worth a damn as they devour
Little by little some sad body in their own cause.

Down, then, with virtue, order, misery;
Down with it all, with it all, saving defeat,
Defeat to the back teeth, to that frozen space
Of a head split asunder by solitude,
In the knowledge that to live is to be alone with death.

Not even to wait for that bird with the arms of a woman,
With the delectably darkened voice of a man,
Because a bird, even when in love,
Is not worth waiting for, as any monarch
Waits for the towers to mature into rotten fruit.

Let us just cry out,
Cry out to a wing entirely,
To collapse so many heavens,
Touching solitude with a preserved hand.

NOCTURNO ENTRE LAS MUSARAÑAS

Cuerpo de piedra, cuerpo triste
Entre lanas con muros de universo,
Idéntico a las razas cuando cumplen años,
A los más inocentes edificios,
A las más pudorosas cataratas,
Blancas como la noche, en tanto la montaña
Despedaza formas enloquecidas,
Despedaza dolores como dedos,
Alegrías como uñas.

No saber dónde ir, dónde volver
Buscando los vientos piadosos
Que destruyen las arrugas del mundo,
Que bendicen los deseos cortados a raíz
Antes de dar su flor,
Su flor grande como un niño.

Los labios quieren esa flor
Cuyo puño, besado por la noche,
Abre las puertas del olvido labio a labio.

NOCTURNE OF THE SHREWS

Body of stone, sad body
Among fleeces with walls of universes,
Identical to races when they come of age,
To the most innocent buildings,
To the most modest cataracts,
White as the night, while the mountain
Shreds crazy pieces,
Shreds pain like fingers,
Joy like fingernails.

Not knowing where to go, where to turn
In search of merciful winds
Which destroy the world's wrinkles,
Which bless uprooted desire
Before it can flourish,
With its flower, big as a child.

Lips love that flower
Whose fist, kissed by the night,
Opens the doors of oblivion lip by lip.

COMO LA PIEL

Ventana huérfana con cabellos habituales,
Gritos del viento,
Atroz paisaje entre cristal de roca,
Prostituyendo los espejos vivos,
Flores clamando a gritos
Su inocencia anterior a obesidades.

Esas cuevas de luces venenosas,
Destrozan los deseos, los durmientes,
Luces como lenguas hendidas
Penetrando en los huesos hasta hallar la carne,
Sin saber que en el fondo no hay fondo,
No hay nada, sino un grito,
Un grito, otro deseo
Sobre una trampa de adormideras crueles

En un mundo de alambre
Donde el olvido vuela por debajo del suelo,
En un mundo de angustia,
Alcohol amarillento,
Plumas de fiebre,
Ira subiendo a un cielo de vergüenza,
Algún día nuevamente resurgirá la flecha
Que abandona el azar
Cuando una estrella muere como otoño para olvidar su sombra.

LIKE SKIN

Orphan window with habitual hairs,
Cries of the wind,
Atrocious landscape among glass of rock,
Prostituting vivid mirrors,
Flowers proclaiming loud
Their former innocence of obesities.

Those caves of venomous lights,
Destroy desires and the sleepers,
Lights like cracked tongues
Penetrating bone until flesh is found,
Without knowing that deep down there is no deep down,
There is nothing, except a cry,
A cry, another desire
On a snare of cruel poppies

In a world of wire
Where oblivion flies underground,
In a world of anguish,
Yellow alcohol,
Fevered plume,
Anger rising to a shameful sky,
Some day there will fly again the arrow
Which abandons chance
When a star dies like autumn to forget its shadow.

NOTES

Remorse in a Dinner Jacket
This poem was written in Toulouse on 15 April, 1929. The first three poems emerged in a six-day spell, immediately after Cernuda's Easter trip to Paris. This one with its lonely, errant protagonist more than stands comparison with T. S. Eliot's *Hollow Men* period.

I Want to be Alone in the South
Toulouse, 20 April, 1929. The title seems to have derived from a song-title of the era. The South referred to here is the southern states of the USA. Line 5 practically offers a definition of Blues music itself with its suggestions of languid, lyrical malaise. Note how in this *locus amoenus* darkness and light are assessed as being of equal beauty.

White Shadows
Toulouse, 21 April, 1929. The title is inspired by *White Shadows of the South Seas,* one of the earliest 'talkie' movies – seen by Cernuda in Paris in 1929, and directed by W. S. Van Dyke and Robert Flaherty (the latter being famed for his *Man of Aran*).

Body in Pain
Toulouse, 29 April, 1929. The most Surreal text in the collection so far, this poem explores the subconscious, through a poetic protagonist seen as a drowning man overcome by immersion in the water.

Exile
Toulouse, 2 May, 1929. This is a classic Outsider text, full of suggestions of alienation, exclusion and so on. It includes an image of one of the ultimate forms of social exclusion: a prostitute touting for clients (lines 9–10).

Nevada
Toulouse, 8 May, 1929. There is a notable gay agendum here, with suggestions of same-on-same contact. The title is almost certainly owed to a 1927 Gary Cooper cowboy film of exactly the same name. As anyone who has ever visited there will know, the state of Nevada is not generally known for its snowy climate.

Like the Wind
Toulouse, 10 May, 1929. Another Outsider poem, notable for its devastating final simile redolent of viciously crushed idealism.

Tell Me Last Night
Toulouse, 19 May, 1929. This is the last of the eight Toulouse poems, and is another quite Surrealist text. The twisted, distorted emotions expressed here are probably attributable, as the reference on line 36 to "despised love" might suggest, to a romantic disappointment.

Total Darkness
Madrid, 2 July, 1929. This poem, evoking lingering emotional despair, is the first of the twenty-two written while Cernuda was residing in Madrid.

The Room Next Door
Madrid, 5 July, 1929. A nightmarish scenario is depicted here; one which, through disconnections worthy of Surrealism (a greyhound, velvet?), seems to underline the sheer meaninglessness of life.

I am Tired
Madrid, 6 July, 1929. The figure of the parrot seems to epitomise languidness and *ennui*. Again this text, shorn of logic and with its seemingly capricious jumble of ideas, verges on the Surreal – although it does not quite go as far down the road of total abandon as prototypical French Surrealism did.

The Case of the Murdered Bird

Madrid, 7 July, 1929. In a sense the final line says all one can say about this enigmatic text. Notable, however, are the uses of the well-known Surrealist formula "color de" ("couleur de") to harness surprising and disjointed elements in an expression. The poem may be read as the reaction to yet another disappointment in love, with Cernuda himself as the vulnerable creature murdered in what amounts to a detective story-like account.

Durango

Madrid, 9 July, 1929. Another of Cernuda's American poems, this text refers to Durango in the USA (and not to the Mexican or Spanish versions). In spite of the allusions to what may be seen as 'butch' and ideal gay archetypal warriors, the poem is typically downbeat in tone and content.

Daytona

Madrid, 11 July, 1929. Here the reader is transported to the coastal Floridian city of Daytona, famous in the 1920s – and still today – for its association with motor-racing. One can imagine that Cernuda derived this location from perhaps a Pathé News-type viewing in a cinema. His evocation of the place again borders on the Surreal, with its catalogue of destruction; the poem also speaks of Cernuda's growing disillusionment with the USA which, initially in his imagination, was some sort of ideal place.

Misery

Madrid, 19 July, 1929. This poem would seem to be about the search for articulation and communication within a love relationship. The wheel of Fortune does not, however, seem to favour the poetic protagonist.

Let's Not Ever Try Love Again

Madrid, 19 July, 1929. The second of two poems written (or finished) in a single day, this one is about another bitter romantic disappointment, leading onto a final nihilistic reflection (comparable to the ending of T. S. Eliot's 1925 poem *The Hollow Men*: "This is the way the world ends / Not with a bang but a whimper").

Red Lantern
Madrid, 27 July, 1929. Compare the words of the Prince of Denmark in Act 2 Scene II of Shakespeare's *Hamlet*: "Then are our beggars' bodies, and our monarchs and outstretched heroes the beggars' shadows".

Scarlet Seas
Madrid, 31 July, 1929. A quite Surrealist poem, which is full of bizarre and incongruous images.

Reason for Tears
Madrid, 6 August, 1929. Here the night is imagined as a prostitute, swinging her hips, waiting for clients on street corners.

All This for Love
Madrid, 6 August, 1929. This is, in some ways, a 'political' poem, in which Cernuda makes plain his distaste for the Spanish monarchy (or, perhaps, indeed any monarchy) founded, as he sees it, on the flimsiest of superficial pretexts: arranged marriage, for example. Despite the destruction of an erotic dream (of the homosexual variety), alluded to here, there is also an implicit expression of the hope for the survival of love.

I Do Not Know What to Call Him in My Dreams
Madrid, 8 August, 1929. This is quite an erotic text, with a definite gay agendum, in which a hope is expressed for the realisation of homoerotic ideals.

Sleep, Sonny
Madrid, 9 August, 1929. This text, along with the next one in the collection, was published in the literary magazine *Nueva revista*, in May 1930, under the title *A Little River. A Little Love*; both were dedicated to Buddy Van Arlen, who appears to have been a Jazzman (or perhaps a movie star), long since forgotten. A bitter, sardonic tone is evident.

Drama or Closed Door
Madrid, 16 August, 1929. A poem wherein a fear factor is articulated.

Leave Me Alone
Madrid, 16 August, 1929. This text includes again the repeated use of the classic Surrealist formula: "color de".

Sea Flesh
Madrid, 18 August, 1929. The disparity between the title and the poem's content is typically surrealistic. This is another 'paradise lost'-type American poem. It has an undoubted musical swing or feel to it; although Cernuda concludes on a harsh note.

Old Riverbank
Madrid, 22 August, 1929. Here, in this poem that touches on a sort of nostalgia for childhood, Cernuda's utter despair is epitomised. Notwithstanding that is the ludic, song-like quality of a line such as verse 7.

The Song of the West
Madrid, 28 August, 1929. A poem (one might say Cernuda's *Brokeback Mountain*) in which he expresses his final and total disillusionment with the USA. The text is replete with Surrealist touches (including the by now familiar "color de" phrase) such as Dalíesque melting, not of clocks, but of hands. Signifier and signified are further apart than ever in this poem which flirts with total absence of meaning. Its jigsaw-like collages eventually boil down to apparent sameness and utter nihilism.

Are They All Happy?
Madrid, 28 August, 1929. Cernuda does not hold back, in this poem with its mocking and ironic title and content, in his scathing criticism of contemporary Spain (that of the Primo de Rivera dictatorship). This overtly political poem also has a gay undertone, and might ultimately be said to express a wish to obliterate the world that destroyed the poet's dreams.

Nocturne of the Shrews
Madrid, 29 August, 1929. Reads like an attempted reconstruction of truly bizarre erotic dreams.

Like Skin
Madrid, 31 August, 1929. This final poem is full of logic-defying Surrealist elements.

www.ingramcontent.com/pod-product-compliance
Lightning Source LLC
Chambersburg PA
CBHW071133100726
47908CB00008B/2590